Grandma Carol's Plant

By Rowena Cory Lindquist
Illustrated by Trish Hill

I

Peter gave Grandma Carol a plant.

Grandma Carol gave Peter a hug. "Thank you, Peter," she said. "I'll try my best to look after it."

Grandma Carol didn't know much about plants, so she borrowed a gardening book from the library.

Early next morning, Grandma Carol
put Peter's plant where it would get
some sunlight. Then she left for work.

But when she came home, the plant looked just the same.

Grandma Carol read the gardening book again. She had forgotten to water Peter's plant!

Early next morning, Grandma Carol
watered Peter's plant.

Then she went to work.

But when she came home, the plant looked just the same.

Grandma Carol read the gardening book again.

Grandma Carol thought the pot
might be too small, so she put Peter's
plant into a bigger pot.

Early next morning, she watered
Peter's plant before going to work.

But when she came home, the plant looked just the same.

Grandma Carol read the gardening book again.

She hadn't given the plant any plant food!

Grandma Carol went to a nursery
and came back with some plant food
for Peter's plant.

Early next morning, Grandma Carol looked at Peter's plant.

"I've watered you," she said. "I've put you in a bigger pot. I've made sure you have plenty of sun and plant food. Why won't you bloom?"

Then she went to work.

But when she came home, the plant looked just the same.

Grandma Carol was sad. "Tomorrow Peter is coming," she said. "He'll be so sad if his plant hasn't bloomed."

The next day, Grandma Carol met
Peter at her front door.

"I'm sorry about your plant, Peter,"
she said. "I have tried everything.
I put your plant in the sun, I watered
it, I put it in a bigger pot, and I
gave it plant food… but it still
wouldn't bloom!"

"I know you have been taking care of it," said Peter. "I've seen the flower on my way to school each day."

Grandma Carol didn't believe him, so Peter took her to look at the plant.

"See, it has bloomed!" said Peter, pointing to the plant.

"But the flower was never open when I looked at it!" said Grandma Carol.

Peter grinned. "That's because it only opens for the sun!" he said.